DIVERSITY PARTNERSHIP TIPS FOR WHITE WOMEN AND PEOPLE OF COLOR TO ENGAGE WHITE MEN: A SKILLS-BUILDING FIELD GUIDE

By: Jo Ann Morris, Bill Proudman and Michael Welp

WMFDP, LLC

WMFDP, LLC
PO Box 12436
Portland, OR 97212
(503) 281-5585

Order books at www.wmfdp.com

ISBN 0-9754192-2-6
Library of Congress Control Number: 2004107090

TESTIMONIALS

"This excellent series, on fostering skill-building in partnership surrounding diversity issues, is practical and relevant for both genders and for interfacing with all races and ages."

Angeles Arrien, Ph.D.
Cultural anthropologist and author of *Working Together* and *The Four-Fold Way*

"Proudman, Welp and Morris have very effectively translated into print their profound work in diversity partnerships. They've described the complex humanity involved in leadership in crisp phrases with great clarity. The reflective questions will surely enable the reader to connect head with heart to truly achieve personal growth in partnering for diversity."

Lars Houmann
Executive Vice President and Chief Operating Officer
Florida Hospital

"My work with WMFDP has been some of the most interesting and informative of my entire professional career. The opportunity to learn and understand who I am as a white male, and all that entails both positive and negative, will help me interact more effectively with everyone."

David Ratcliffe
CEO
Southern Company

TESTIMONIALS

"These field guides on Partnership in Diversity address the chasm separating millions of white men from their natural allies in creating inclusive relationships, groups, organizations, and communities. They point the way with clear examples and models that will inform and promote deep understanding and collaboration in the pursuit of social justice."

Charlie Seashore and Edie Seashore
Recipients of the Lifetime Achievement Awards of the Organization Development Network

CONTENTS

ACKNOWLEDGMENTS

Many people helped us in the creation of this field guide. Foremost we thank our clients, whose partnership has helped us shape and evolve our ideas. Our appreciation also goes to our associates, who share our passion, support our ongoing growth and help us proudly serve our clients. Special thanks to our business partner Tim McNichol who challenged and supported the evolution of our work. Thanks also to Donna Ginn, Peggy McIntosh, Nancy Brown, and Mark Chesler for reviewing this text and providing valuable feedback.

INTRODUCTION TO THE WMFDP FIELD GUIDE SERIES

White Men as Full Diversity Partners® (WMFDP, LLC) is a company driven by a desire to change the way diversity is practiced in the United States. We believe that building effective diversity partnerships creates critical leadership skills that have often been absent from most organizations' leadership development and diversity initiatives. We believe diversity partnerships leverage leadership skills and can be developed throughout an organization.

We are pursuing three goals in the establishment of diversity partnerships and inclusive organizations:

1] The first goal is the automatic inclusion of white men and their diversity rather than including everyone else but white men.

2] The second is the inclusion of work that women and men of color, and white women are invited to do to examine how their assumptions, interactions, and experiences influence their diversity partnerships with white men as well as their interactions with each other.

3] The third is the ability of leaders to see and act on the symbiotic relationship between leadership skill development and the creation of diversity partnerships. Linking leadership and diversity partnerships on a daily basis can transform mindsets and build skills. The results are courageous actions that benefit people and the goals of their organizations.

It doesn't matter to us what position you hold. What does matter is that all of us have work to do and a role to play in changing the way diversity is practiced and valued.

This field guide is a companion to another guide for white men, which outlines the work they need to do to create breakthrough diversity partnerships, and a third field guide which focuses on the eight critical leadership skills developed through diversity partnership work. This guide was written to support you. In order to benefit, you will need to take action: read, reflect on the questions, experiment with the activities, and apply the insights to your work and life. Use this guide to increase your understanding of diversity, your leadership ability, and your diversity partnership skills. Your actions today and tomorrow are what count.

The partners and associates of WMFDP, LLC are grateful for our clients' courageous actions and persistence in doing the work that creates diversity partnerships and makes inclusive organizations a reality.

WHO SHOULD USE THIS FIELD GUIDE?

This field guide focuses on the practice and refinement of diversity partnership skills. It is written in a conversational tone and speaks directly to you the reader. Anyone who wants to learn more about partnerships and what it takes to build and sustain them can use and benefit from this field guide. Specifically, the guide is intended for:

- Business leaders and managers
- Diversity councils and employee networks
- Individuals and groups in for-profit and non-profit organizations
- Professors and their students

How to Use This Field Guide

This is a "take-action" field guide. It is designed for you to use interactively – at work, in your community and your personal life. No field guide works in the same way for any two people, so we have included a variety of ways to look at the topics explored in the field guide.

Historically, white women and people of color have done almost all of the work of educating white men on diversity issues. Transforming this dynamic – such that white men, white women, and women and men of color partner together effectively – is not effortless, but it is possible. Pursuing diversity partnership work requires new ways of thinking and new behaviors. All of the field guides were written to help you do the work; the choice is yours.

The first half of this field guide introduces tips, skill descriptions and reflective questions to help you apply the skills described.

The second section provides activities to further develop these skills. Some of the activities can be done individually, while others are suggested for group work. Work with each tip, or strategy, and use the field guide to push yourself further out onto your learning edge.

While these guides primarily address issues related to race and gender, many of the tips and questions are applicable to other kinds of difference; for example, sexual orientation, age and economic background. These diversity partnerships are also key to organizational health and business success.

Some helpful suggestions when using this field guide:

1] The intent of the field guide is to help you become more conscious and competent in the development and application of diversity partnership skills. It takes perseverance and practice. Don't expect perfection or immediate results.

2] Work alone and with others. Find ways to work with colleagues and/or friends. This work is about partnership and reflection. You might begin with solo reflection by answering questions you find in the field guide. Your next step might be to ask a colleague or friend to work with you. Have them act as a coach or mentor, someone to talk through how you are putting into action the tip or skill you chose.

3] Don't attempt to read through the field guide cover to cover. Take it one small chunk at a time. Read through each tip and work the one that appeals to you the most. Work with one reflective question at a time.

4] Take notes. Notice what is easy and makes sense and where you become confused and/or resistant. Use your coach to talk through those spots and seek learning that brings *immediate* relevancy to your diversity partnership efforts at work.

5] Acknowledge and celebrate each small step forward in strengthening your partnership skills practice. If you feel stuck in one spot, move onto another tip or reflective question.

6] This field guide is an entry into a variety of partnership strategies, not an exhaustive list. Approach the study of diversity partnership the way an anthropologist would go on a dig. Look at things from different angles. Be curious. Ask questions. Write your own reflective questions. Suspend judgment.

As you deepen your practice of diversity partnership we invite you to tell us what you are learning. Share reflective questions that you created by using this field guide. Your insights will help direct subsequent revisions of the guide. Email your comments and additions to **fieldguides@wmfdp.com**

Based on our experiences with a wide range of clients, if you commit to this skill-building adventure, you'll discover more choices in how you relate to and interact with others. You will become more aware of how you are developing and using your skills and resources in new ways. You will also be more equipped to use them in creating effective and satisfying partnerships built on shared understanding, whether at work or at home.

REFLECTIONS FROM OUR CLIENTS

"Seeing others sit with difficult conversations helps me stay with it and build muscle
and resiliency in my own attempts at partnership."

"When I look at what's up for me at work right now that requires partnership,
I'm questioning how to create the powerful results we created here, with my group."

"I live with a chronic stress I didn't know I had (as a woman and a person of color)."

"It helps to know what the shared vision of the outcome is for a partnership
and my stake in it."

"Turbulence has an important place in my partnership work. I must remember
to invite it in."

UNDERSTAND
WHAT IS IN IT FOR YOU

I f asked, how would you describe what is in it for you, men and women of color and white women, to have more white men as full diversity partners? Your answers to this question and the ones below can help you identify areas in need of change within your organization. Your choices and actions can affect change. Some changes you identify may not happen without you.

TIP 1 AS SKILL:

- *I see diversity partnerships as vital to the day-to-day work I am responsible to perform.*

- *Doing so changes the way I interact with people and how I go about making decisions which affect them, whether or not I am in a leadership position.*

- *I make diversity partnership and its responsibilities a regular staff meeting agenda item, or I raise the need for it at meetings I attend. I am specific about the positive business implications that result from it and its benefit to me professionally and personally. I report specific examples and their impact.*

- *I question the efficacy of the company building partnerships across the many differences represented by our customers, vendors and surrounding communities. I do this when the company seems to under-value the same important diversity partnerships inside the company.*

- *I apply the leadership skills of Leveraging Ambiguity and Turbulence* and Integrating Head and Heart* as I make and implement leadership decisions.*

* See *Eight Critical Leadership Skills Created Through Effective Diversity Partnerships*, WMFDP, LLC

REFLECTIVE QUESTIONS:

1] What are the benefits to me and/or others in being a "full diversity partner" with white men? What are the costs to me and/or others in not doing diversity partnership work with white men?

_____

_____

_____

_____

_____

_____

_____

_____

_____

_____

_____

_____

2] How might I change my attitudes and behavior in support of white men being my diversity partners? What results might I create?

_____

_____

_____

_____

_____

_____

_____

_____

_____

_____

_____

_____

3] What lessons or insights have I learned from people I view as different from me that I would find difficult to be without today?

_____

_____

_____

_____

_____

_____

_____

4] How have these lessons and insights influenced my leadership skills, partnering skills, and/or my ability to perform?

_____

_____

_____

_____

_____

_____

_____

5] How do I know that I am a trusted diversity partner/leader? What behaviors and actions are exhibited by the diversity partners/leaders I trust?

_____

_____

_____

_____

_____

_____

_____

USE AN INQUIRY APPROACH

D on't assume that you know a white man's diversity journey. Ask questions that can help you discover how diversity was and is a part of his life. Ask him to describe his journey and current diversity challenges. Tell him about your journey. Ask what you can stop, start and continue to do to increase his willingness to engage you as a diversity partner. Acknowledge the work he has done and the ways he identifies himself as an ally or diversity partner. Don't forget to ask about his willingness to engage in diversity dialogues with you.

TIP 2 AS SKILL:

- *I ask others about their diversity experiences and journeys, rather than telling them my interpretations of their journeys based on my assumptions.*

- *I drop my preconceived ideas about white men and acknowledge that each experience with any of my partners is but one experience.*

- *I stop silencing myself, my white male partners and others by acting as if I have all the answers about who they are as peers, managers and leaders…regardless of my past experiences with them.*

- *I examine my grievances and/or my suspicions about white men (and other partners) that were formed by past experience. I ignore those that bear little or no resemblance to my current partnerships.*

- *If there are leftovers, I examine them aloud with the appropriate partner as a way to discover the truth and strengthen our partnership as a result. I use the leadership skills of Managing Difficult Conversations* and Listening* to accomplish this.*

* See *Eight Critical Leadership Skills Created Through Effective Diversity Partnerships*, WMFDP, LLC

REFLECTIVE QUESTIONS:

1] How are my diversity partnerships with white men improving the quality of my work with others day to day?

_____

_____

_____

_____

_____

_____

_____

_____

_____

_____

_____

2] When asked, what do white men say they need from me in order to be full diversity partners in support of business goals?

_____

_____

_____

_____

_____

_____

_____

_____

_____

_____

_____

3] How do I know I listen closely to their responses? How does my reflection on what is asked of me, help me to tell them what I can reasonably do and why?

_____

_____

_____

_____

_____

_____

_____

_____

_____

_____

_____

4] How might I emphasize the positive results of diversity partnership work on business results?

_____

_____

_____

_____

_____

_____

_____

_____

_____

_____

_____

_____

ONE WHITE MAN IS NOT WHITE MALE CULTURE

L earn to separate white male culture* from the actions and behaviors of individual white men. They, like you, have been conditioned to operate in, and are affected by, this culture. Look for ways to notice the different effects of this culture both on them and on you. Make the results of the culture – positive and negative – visible to all without putting individuals on trial or holding them personally responsible for systemic injustices. Notice what you and white men are doing to uncover and acknowledge systemic injustices within your organization. By their very nature, systemic injustices can be so interwoven in the fabric of how things are done in business cultures that they have become institutionalized, and therefore, are harder to see.

* See more on Euro-American or American white male culture in the appendix.

TIP 3 AS SKILL:

- *I ask questions about what it means to be white and male, rather than assume I know.*

- *I accept that the white man I am interacting with is unique, as is his point of view.*

- *In dialogues with a white man, I ask myself what it is I want, besides understanding. I examine my intentions. Am I having this conversation to support partnership and our work together or to somehow provide him with the experience of having his culture scrutinized?*

- *I listen to understand what he says that confirms and/or refutes my stereotypes about white male culture.*

- *I explore white male culture with him to discover how much he is aware of it and what about it he accepts or rejects.*

- *Together we identify how he demonstrates acceptance and/or rejection of white male culture at work, and how either could impact on our ability to be effective partners/leaders. I apply the leadership skill of Listening* to demonstrate my respect for his perspectives on white male culture.*

* See *Eight Critical Leadership Skills Created Through Effective Diversity Partnerships*, WMFDP, LLC

REFLECTIVE QUESTIONS:

1] What do I really know about what it means to be white and male? How might this
be different than what I think I know about the experiences of white women
and women and men of color at work?

_____

_____

_____

_____

_____

_____

_____

_____

_____

_____

2] What do I value about the white men I work with or other white men in my life?
How many of these things have I purposefully shared with them?

_____

_____

_____

_____

_____

_____

_____

_____

_____

_____

_____

3] How might sharing what I value about white men change my diversity partnerships with them?

_____

_____

_____

_____

_____

_____

_____

_____

_____

_____

_____

_____

4] In what ways do I exhibit attributes of white male culture? Which of these aspects might I have assimilated to the point that I think, "that's just how I am?"

_____

_____

_____

_____

_____

_____

_____

_____

_____

_____

_____

_____

TIP 4

DON'T DO THE WORK
FOR WHITE MEN

Don't allow white men to become dependent on you as their teacher and guide. Tell white men what you need from full diversity partners and hold them accountable. Ask them to hold you accountable to the same standards. Be willing to point out when you think you are being used as a crutch. As a partner, you need to know what you want white men to do that will demonstrate that they are learning and applying that learning at work. Your explicit standards for an ongoing authentic partnership will keep you out of the role of crutch.

TIP 4 AS SKILL:

- *I publicly acknowledge my belief that white men know a great deal about diversity and by doing that, I debunk the myth that they are "clueless."*

- *I regularly point out specific examples of their knowledge and the actions they take as a result. I do this to: support their recognition of the depth of their understanding of diversity issues, explore how our personal diversity journeys differ, and acknowledge where there are similarities.*

- *I behave in ways that broadcast to others that white men's assumptions, understanding, opinions and perceptions about today's diversity issues - which confront the leaders of organizations large and small – are as valuable to building breakthrough diversity partnerships as are my own.*

- *I do not rescue white men from potentially uncomfortable learning. I do not set myself up as being the answer person. I challenge them to do their own research, discovery and reflection.*

- *I ask my diversity partners to agree on a partnership framework that will limit the likelihood of my being seen and/or used as a crutch for white men's learning.*

REFLECTIVE QUESTIONS:

1] What do I want white men to do that will demonstrate their learning and that they are applying it at work?

_____

_____

_____

_____

_____

_____

_____

_____

_____

_____

_____

_____

2] What are my standards for an ongoing authentic diversity partnership?

_____

_____

_____

_____

_____

_____

_____

_____

_____

_____

_____

3] What is it that I need to know about aspects of my partner's diversity to be more competent in working with him?

_____

_____

_____

_____

_____

_____

_____

4] In what ways do my white male partners lean on me for learning rather than experimenting on their own? What can I suggest that they do instead?

_____

_____

_____

_____

_____

_____

_____

5] Is the framework for my partnerships clear to potential and existing partners? What else do I need to do to clarify it?

_____

_____

_____

_____

_____

_____

_____

A SAMPLE CRUTCH-FREE DIVERSITY PARTNERSHIP FRAMEWORK: A PARTNERSHIP-BUILDING RESOURCE

1] Our respective roles are clear. We ask in order to understand, rather than assuming the other's meaning.

2] We agree on how we will resolve conflict.

3] We use frequent direct feedback about what works in the partnership and what doesn't work. We listen to understand. We talk about how our contributions to each other affect our commitment to our work.

4] We acknowledge the steps we've taken to support and challenge each other. We recognize that our diversity partners may have very different views and understandings of the issues we are facing together. We acknowledge that our frames of reference have been affected by differences of gender, race, class, sexual orientation, experience, etc. It's our job to understand each other's world views and how they influence our work together.

5] We show respect for each other in the moment…when it counts. Some of these moments will occur when we are not together. These will be opportunities we can use to demonstrate respect for each other and our partnership.

6] We attend to a broken trust between us, rather than assume all is lost. "Once broken, never regained" is unacceptable as our first response. Tears in the fabric of our partnership are used to test our commitment, demonstrate tenacity and build skill. We refuse to hold on to misunderstandings. Instead, we schedule time to air and resolve them.

7] We actively apply the key paradoxes.* Individually, we take time to find out whether our perspectives match, or not. We look at how each of us uses the paradoxes and how we demonstrate them in our behavior.

*See appendix for paradox descriptions

YOUR WORDS MAY NOT BE HEARD

That's right. Your words may not be heard as you meant them. Many white men don't see themselves as members of a white male group or as having a culture. They may fail to understand that they or their actions have any connection to a white male group or a white male culture. Work to help white men hear you when you are speaking about them as individuals, as a member of a white male group, or as exhibiting attributes of white male culture. Be clear about the difference.

TIP 5 AS SKILL:

- *I know the stereotypes I hold about white men.*

- *I know how my stereotypes may be operating to cloud my understanding of individual white men.*

- *I do not attribute the behavior of one white man to all white men as a group. I combat assumptions about my ability to partner with white men by exposing my stereotypes of them.*

- *I explain to them how their behavior refutes and/or confirms my stereotypes.*

- *I explore their responses with them, in the moment, as a sign of partnership.*

- *I apply the leadership skill of Courage* to be open to outcomes and continue the dialogue as a means of strengthening our diversity partnership. I support our partnership by hearing how they see themselves and by hearing their thoughts about being seen by others as members of a white male group.*

Whether white men see themselves as individuals and/or as a member of a white male group depends on their understanding of the "individual – group paradox." For more on this paradox and others, see the paradox concept in the appendix.

* See *Eight Critical Leadership Skills Created Through Effective Diversity Partnerships*, WMFDP, LLC

REFLECTIVE QUESTIONS:

1] How do my reactions to the possibility that I won't be heard by white men support and/or limit my desire and ability to be their diversity partner?

_____

_____

_____

_____

_____

_____

_____

_____

_____

_____

_____

_____

2] In what ways can I stay open to white men's realities and so understand them more fully – rather than judge them from my frame of reference?

_____

_____

_____

_____

_____

_____

_____

_____

_____

_____

3] How has my display of emotionality and rationality affected my diversity partnerships with white men and other diversity partners? How has white men's display of emotionality and rationality affected me?

_____

_____

_____

_____

_____

_____

_____

_____

_____

_____

_____

_____

4] When I am not feeling heard by white men, how do I respond? Might my response help or hinder the diversity partnership I am attempting to build?

_____

_____

_____

_____

_____

_____

_____

_____

_____

_____

_____

WHITE MEN ARE OUR ALLIES

Recognize that the vast majority of white men are willing allies who remain unaware that their actions, behaviors and decisions may be at issue. Often this unawareness is also unconscious and prevents them from seeing and examining the potential systemic impacts of their behavior, actions and decisions. They often do not understand the ramifications of their lack of awareness and its effects on partnering with women and men of color and white women, or on how their contributions are valued by the organization as a result of this lack of awareness.

TIP 6 AS SKILL:

- *I recognize my white male allies/partners for the work they do to strengthen our partnerships. I do this frequently and in a variety of ways. I do this privately and publicly as is appropriate to the situation.*

- *I am specific in giving appreciative feedback to white men so they know what to stop, start and continue doing to begin and/or maintain a partnership with me.*

- *I can both support and challenge white men without jeopardizing my partnerships with them.*

- *I point out specific commonalities and disparities in our leadership styles, the ways we handle conflict, come to decisions, etc., in support of our "full diversity partnerships."*

- *I challenge myself to apply the leadership skill of Balancing Key Paradoxes* to assess the difference between a problem and the paradoxes my partners and I can manage together.*

* See *Eight Critical Leadership Skills Created Through Effective Diversity Partnerships*, WMFDP, LLC

REFLECTIVE QUESTIONS:

1] What are my experiences of white men I work with or for? In what ways are they allies? In what ways do they demonstrate diversity partnership? What are the differences between the two, if any?

_____

_____

_____

_____

_____

_____

_____

_____

_____

_____

2] What actions or behaviors from white men invite me into a diversity partnership? Which of those actions/ behaviors do I exhibit to do the same? Which of their actions and behaviors surprised me at first, caused concern and/or skepticism?

_____

_____

_____

_____

_____

_____

_____

_____

_____

_____

_____

3] How do diversity partnership behaviors from white men support the best of white male culture and our partnership?

_____

_____

_____

_____

_____

_____

_____

4] What do women and men of color and white women I work with say or do to represent their willingness to be my partners? Which of their actions and behaviors surprised me at first, caused concern and/or skepticism?

_____

_____

_____

_____

_____

_____

_____

5] What barriers to diversity leadership and authentic diversity partnerships might I have discovered in my answers to the previous questions? What do I want to do about them, if anything?

_____

_____

_____

_____

_____

_____

_____

EXAMINE HOW YOUR ASSUMPTIONS STOP YOU

O ur assumptions and previous experiences can and sometimes do get in our way of being better diversity partners/allies to white men. The skills needed to overcome or quiet our assumptions are the ability to examine, confront and to move past operating from these old assumptions and experiences.

TIP 7 AS SKILL:

- *I am aware of how I talk about white men when not in their company.*

- *I question and confront what assumptions lie beneath the things I say.*

- *I ask others what assumptions they hear in what I say about white men generally and specifically.*

- *I ask for help from others to point out what in my behavior, language, and actions support effective partnership with white men (and others).*

- *I also ask others to point out my behaviors, words, and actions that have the potential to limit partnership with white men (and others). I ask for feedback that acknowledges how I am demonstrating any of the eight critical leadership skills I have been attempting to practice.* *

* See *Eight Critical Leadership Skills Created Through Effective Diversity Partnerships*, WMFDP, LLC

REFLECTIVE QUESTIONS:

1] What assumptions about white men am I unknowingly operating from? How might I find out about them? What am I willing to do about them once I know?

_____

_____

_____

_____

_____

_____

_____

_____

_____

_____

_____

2] How might my assumptions silence me or in some other way influence my partnerships with white men (and others)? What are the results?

_____

_____

_____

_____

_____

_____

_____

_____

_____

_____

_____

_____

3] How might what I say to others about my feelings, thoughts and actions toward white men affect my partnerships with those who observe me? How might what I say affect their partnerships with white men?

_____

_____

_____

_____

_____

_____

_____

_____

_____

_____

_____

_____

4] What might others be learning about my attitudes/assumptions about white men? Why might it benefit me to know?

_____

_____

_____

_____

_____

_____

_____

_____

_____

_____

_____

ASSIST WOMEN AND PEOPLE OF COLOR

First, deliver the message that diversity partnership work is not about when-white-men-get-it-everything-will-get-better. Leaders know that women and men of color, and white women, have their own work to do in order to create breakthrough diversity partnerships. Help them use their knowledge and experience, and interpersonal and leadership skills, to form breakthrough diversity partnerships with each other and with white men.

Be aware of how you collude to keep white men at a distance and/or comfortable. Your colleagues may be able to list how you pay lip service to the idea of diversity partnership. Can you? Are you cognizant of how your unspoken attitudes towards white men affect your relationships with them, women and men of color, and white women? Consider the questions below to discover how your attitudes and assumptions about white men play a part in not only how your partnerships with them develop, but also in the quality of the business results you create with them.

TIP 8 AS SKILL:

- *I acknowledge and support women and men of color, and white women who work to ease and/or heighten the tensions which exist within and between various identity groups in organizations, as appropriate.*

- *I tell my co-workers, peers and leaders how their comments and behavior toward white men influence my perceptions of them as leaders and diversity partners. I ask them about the experiences that shape their opinions and assumptions about white men.*

- *I explore and support their willingness to create breakthrough diversity partnerships with each other and with white men. I question disparities between what they say and what they do to build partnerships with each other and with white men.*

- *I support them to identify the perceived cost of confronting politically correct behavior – mine and their own – which limits organizational inclusiveness and trust-based diversity partnerships.*

REFLECTIVE QUESTIONS:

1] What myths and positive stereotypes about white men do I hold that affect the way I view women and men of color, and white women, as diversity partners?

_____

_____

_____

_____

_____

_____

_____

_____

_____

_____

_____

2] What myths and positive stereotypes about women and men of color and white women am I operating from? How would it assist us to engage in a dialogue about our myths and stereotypes about each other?

_____

_____

_____

_____

_____

_____

_____

_____

_____

_____

_____

_____

3] If I operated from a place of unconditional acceptance of white men as my full diversity partners, how would my behavior and actions change towards them, women and men of color, and white women?

_____

_____

_____

_____

_____

_____

_____

_____

_____

_____

_____

4] How do I react to the suggestion that attention be given to white men's diversity struggles? What assumptions are operating for me that might contribute to my reactions? How do my reactions invite, limit, and/or deepen my diversity partnerships?

_____

_____

_____

_____

_____

_____

_____

_____

_____

_____

_____

ASSIST WHITE MEN

Y ou can assist white men by contributing to their understanding of their own self-interest in being full diversity partners. You can point out what they can gain from doing partnership work. When you see them demonstrate diversity partnership behavior toward other white men, men and women of color, and white women, or when they express it toward you, help make what they do and its influence visible to them. You can also point out what you think they lose if they take the stance that there is no benefit to them in becoming full diversity partners.

TIP 9 AS SKILL:

- *I tell them my truth. I listen to theirs with compassion and patience.*

- *I do my own work of uncovering why I act as I do toward white men.*

- *I use a partnership framework that spells out what I hope for from the partnership as well as what will make it work for me. I ask my partners to do the same.*

- *I acknowledge white men for their work on understanding their own diversity.*

- *I applaud the risks white men take on behalf of their diversity partnerships, including their partnerships with other white men.*

- *I describe how my work benefits from my diversity partnerships.*

- *I give white men the benefit of the doubt by resisting the "there they go again" types of responses that limit the development of breakthrough diversity partnerships with them and others.*

REFLECTIVE QUESTIONS:

1] What tells me that my diversity partners understand my intentions?

_____

_____

_____

_____

_____

_____

_____

2] Which of my behaviors and actions make me less effective in my partnerships with white men?

_____

_____

_____

_____

_____

_____

_____

3] Which of their behaviors and actions do I respond to in a way that makes me less effective?

_____

_____

_____

_____

_____

_____

_____

4] When I am feeling frozen or stuck in my partnerships with white men, what might I ask them and others to do to help me move forward?

_____

_____

_____

_____

_____

_____

_____

5] When I put questions of guilt and innocence aside, what new options emerge for me to assist white men?

_____

_____

_____

_____

_____

_____

_____

6] How might new options to assist white men offer all diversity partners leadership development opportunities or ways to move toward an inclusive partnership culture?

_____

_____

_____

_____

_____

_____

_____

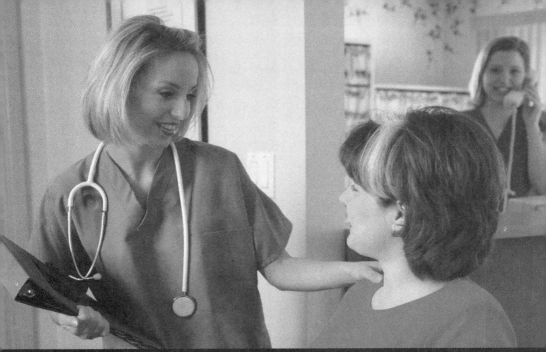

USING SUPPORT SYSTEMS CAN KEEP YOU ALIVE

Locate or create a support system for yourself. Don't try to take on this diversity partnership work alone, even though some of it starts with you. Building and maintaining breakthrough diversity partnerships can be exacting work. There is no good reason to do it alone. Stay in a learning stance. Continually support yourself. Any work can be wearing when you are overly tired, skipped lunch, didn't get to the gym or have not had time alone or with friends to re-energize.

The Power of 5 by Harold H. Bloomfield, M.D., and Robert K. Cooper, Ph.D., offers actions you can take that range from five seconds to five minutes that can help you establish time-saving ways to provide you the fuel you need to support you being at your best. You might even have some fun while you are at it!

TIP 10 AS SKILL:

- *I seek out and spend time with people who are known for their leadership on diversity issues and who have a reputation for being trusted diversity partners, regardless of their level in the organization.*

- *I join employee networks or interest groups that support the development of diversity partnership skills.*

- *I attend skill development experiences that expand my leadership abilities and my network of potential support contacts.*

- *I schedule time for reflection to assimilate new insights and to renew my commitment to building quality diversity partnerships.*

- *I stay in touch with diversity partners from previous organizations and projects.*

- *I form support relationships within perceived sameness and across differences.*

- *I recognize and respect my own and others' needs to change their priorities, to maintain an appropriate balance between being in the lead on diversity issues and stepping back to observe and rest.*

REFLECTIVE QUESTIONS:

1] What form of support system might be of value to me?

_____

_____

_____

_____

_____

_____

_____

2] How can I apply what I know now about diversity and partnership that I did not know months/years ago, to new partnerships?

_____

_____

_____

_____

_____

_____

_____

3] Which employee networks might provide the support I need right now? What other groups come to mind, in or outside of the company, where I can get the support I need?

_____

_____

_____

_____

_____

_____

_____

4] Who are my most trusted allies/partners? How might they be able to support me? If I haven't gone to them already, why not? If I have, are they the right people to provide what I need? Why? Why not?

_____

_____

_____

_____

_____

_____

_____

_____

_____

_____

5] What steps do I need to take this week to begin to build a support system that works for me?

_____

_____

_____

_____

_____

_____

_____

_____

_____

_____

_____

ACTIVITIES

ACTIVITY 1

A DAY IN THE LIFE

ACTIVITY 2

MY WORDS, THEIR MESSAGE

ACTIVITY 3

A PLACE TO START

ACTIVITY 4

FRACTURED FABLES

ACTIVITY 5

QUICK DIVERSITY PARTNERSHIP ASSESSMENT

ACTIVITY 6

IT HAPPENS EVERYDAY

A DAY IN THE LIFE

GOALS:

To discover how your experience of a typical day at work may be similar and different from your peers.

To discover important similarities and differences between how you and others operate in the work setting.

To consider the costs of any differences and/or similarities you discover.

To examine the positive and negative affects of any differences and/or similarities you discover.
Time Needed: 1-2 Hours

STEPS:

1] Write a short description of your day at work. Include who you see, how you are treated, your behavior in meetings, your level of satisfaction with your contributions, how you are treated by others, etc.

2] Read your description aloud.

3] Choose someone you've seen or know at work. Imagine that s/he now has your current job. Write another description but this time write about how their day might be the same and/or different.

4] Compare the two descriptions. What do you notice? What stands out? Discuss your descriptions with a person with whom you share at least two of the same dimensions of diversity. Record what you learn from the discussion. How will you apply what you learn to your diversity partnerships and to the decisions you make at work?

5] Take note of how the comparison of the descriptions highlights issues that might have been invisible to you before. What might the comparison say about situations at work that may be occurring around you? What areas require your attention and leadership?

6] Talk to two or three people, who lead on diversity issues, about your findings. Describe what you discovered and ask for their perspectives. Note any new learning and actions that result from this activity.

VARIATION 2 — IN PARTNERSHIP

Invite a white male colleague to do steps 1-4 with you, where you each record your own experience, then compare. Ask your partner in the activity to share his insights with you. Then explore together: "What might change in this organization if everyone did this activity?" Record what you learn about how the way one sees and experiences things at work changes given race, gender and or other aspects of diversity.

VARIATION 2 — LEADERSHIP MEETING

This activity can be used at a diversity leadership meeting as an opener, or as an exercise at a business operations offsite.
Estimated Time: 1 Hour

STEPS:

1] 15 minutes to write the first and second descriptions.

2] 15 minutes in pairs to share and discuss the descriptions from each person.

3] 5 minutes in same pair to record five insights from doing the activity together.

4] 10 minutes to record insights from all pairs.

5] 15 minutes to discuss the impact of the group's insights.

6] Leave each participant with the inquiry: What are the implications for us and our organization?

VARIATION 3 — DIVERSITY CONFERENCE WORKSHOP

Estimated time: 90 minutes

STEPS:

1-4] Same as in the Leadership Meeting variation.
5] Discuss impacts in groups of 5-6 for 20 minutes.
6] Large group discussion for remaining time about one thing each person
will do to apply the insights from the workshop back at work and/or with
friends and family.

MY WORDS, THEIR MESSAGE

GOALS:

To discover how white men hear what I say to them – do they hear me speaking to them as an individual or as a representative of "the white male group?"

To discover intentions I may not hear when I speak to white men at work.

To understand how negative and positive perceptions of white men as a group may enter into my conversations/work with individuals, without my conscious awareness.
Estimated Time: A workday

STEPS:

1] Keep track of what you say to white men throughout the day. Get a small notepad or create a folder in your PDA for this experiment.

2] Take five minutes after interactions with white men to record the gist of your interactions with specific attention to the tone of your responses. Capture your feelings and thoughts, particularly any of your thoughts that you chose not to express. Ask yourself why you didn't express them and what the long-term result of your silence might be. Remember, no more than five minutes.

3] Have a few short follow-up dialogues with some of the white men and ask each what he heard and how he took it. Talk with him about what he might have heard that you weren't aware of broadcasting. You are not looking for positives or negatives. What you are after is his experience of the interaction, whatever it was.

4] Record what you learn, how will you apply it and actions you will take.

VARIATION:

Estimated time: 30 - 45 minutes

STEPS:

1] Make a list of the top five things you need from white men in order to strengthen your diversity partnerships with them.

2] Ask a white male colleague to do the same (five things he needs from you).

3] Share your lists.

4] Ask him what he heard during the conversation that let him know that you were relating to him as an individual. Find out if he heard things he perceived as your reacting to him as a representative of the white male group.

5] Commit to each other how each of you will do what the other requested.

A PLACE TO START

Not knowing the questions to ask about white men's diversity journeys can hamper dialogue intended to help you and others explore this territory. A Place to Start is an activity that can supply you with enough questions for several different opportunities to learn and lead.

GOALS:

To invite dialogue that explores the diversity journeys of white men.

To develop understanding of white men's diversity journeys and the impact of sharing their journeys with coworkers.

To include white men's diversity journeys in the overall fabric of organizational diversity.

To increase the awareness of women and men of color and white women about how their perceptions of white men's diversity journeys differ from and/or agree with the reality white men report.

Estimated Time: 1-3 Hours if all steps are done on the same day

STEPS:

1] Work with two or three people (including at least one white man) to brainstorm a list of questions that have the potential to illicit information about white men's diversity journeys. Explain the steps of the activity. Disband the brainstorm group after the brainstorm is over (15-20 minutes) and remind them that you will share what you learn with them.

Sample questions:
What was the first incident you remember that told you that you were different from the other children in your neighborhood?

On your first trip away from home as a young adult, perhaps in your 20s, might you remember someone that stood out as very different from anyone you had known before?

What did you learn from him or her?

2] Identify three or four white men to interview using the brainstorm list.

3] Conduct at least three 30-minute interviews using the questions. You can do all of the interviews right after the questions are generated on the same day or you can do one interview a week. Decide on a timing that works best for you, given your work load.

4] Document your learning after each interview.

5] Share your interview data with the brainstorm group.

VARIATION

Share your learning with a diversity network group.

FRACTURED FABLES

GOALS:
To identify invisible myths, assumptions and opinions about white men that affect your partnerships with them.

To assess the affect of myths, assumptions and opinions on building effective diversity partnerships with white men, women and men of color, and white women.
Estimated Time: 30 to 90 minutes

STEPS:
1] Write a fable about what you believe, think and/or feel about white men.

2] Read and discuss your fable with a white man. Notice if during the conversation the fable is fractured or if something about the conversation is helping to strengthen the fable's hold on you.

3] Repeat step 2 with a woman and/or man of color.

4] Compare the outcomes of both conversations and note what you discovered from each one.

5] Experiment with the fable for one work day by interacting with white men as if the fable were fractured – meaning it is no longer true or influences your interactions with white men.

6] Debrief the results of the activity and what you learned with both of the people with whom you initially shared the fable.

VARIATION
Repeat steps 1-6 substituting another aspect of diversity (white women, men and women of color, gays, lesbians, transgendered people, age, class, personality type, etc.)

QUICK DIVERSITY PARTNER ASSESSMENT

GOALS:

To provide diversity partners a quick way to take the pulse of their partnership.

To give diversity partners an opportunity to compare their original expectations of the partnership with their current expectations.

To identify what's working and what isn't.

To give diversity partners opportunities to compare their experiences of the partnership.

To provide opportunities for diversity partners to discover what each needs to do to strengthen their partnership.

To provide opportunities for diversity partners to acknowledge what each does to sustain their partnership.

Estimated Time: 45 minutes

STEPS:

1] Review the expectations you had at the beginning of your partnership.

2] Examine if your expectations were met. How? If not, why not?

3] Tell your diversity partner one thing you gain from the partnership. Describe how you can apply something you are learning or a skill you are honing because of the partnership to others. Describe how the partnership helps you contribute even more to your work and business goals.

4] Decide if more time is needed to discuss anything that feels unresolved.

5] Schedule another quick assessment within 30 days.

QUICK DIVERSITY PARTNER ASSESSMENT

VARIATION 1
Substitute some of the following questions during your assessment:

1] What were my feelings when I began this partnership?

2] What are my feelings now?

3] What unresolved conflicts might we be avoiding, or that might need to be addressed today?

4] How do we handle conflict when it arises?

VARIATION 2
Identify how this quick assessment could be applied to other aspects of your work as a leader.

VARIATION 3
Substitute statement completions as another way to assess the health of your diversity partnership. Add your own statements to the samples below.

1] Something I've contributed to this partnership is _____

2] Something we have achieved together is _____

3] Something I assumed about you is _____

4] Now that I know you prefer _____ , I _____

5] I stopped _____ so you could _____

6] I now know the importance of _____ because our partnership _____

IT HAPPENS EVERYDAY

You are in another meeting and once again a colleague is repeatedly interrupted and their ideas go unheard. You notice that they stop contributing and leave as soon as the meeting is over without touching base with anyone. This scenario is so well known that it is almost a cliché. Why does this continue to happen and what do you do? How can you interrupt this and other patterns of behavior that have a direct, negative affect on performance?

GOALS:

To expose patterns that have negative affects on performance and the effectiveness of diversity partnerships.

To engage in difficult conversations with skill (one-on-one and/or with a group).

To create commitment to change behaviors that limit employee participation and contributions.
Estimated Time: 30-45 minutes

STEPS:

1] 15 minutes – Prepare your Pattern Script (below P1-P7) and practice going through it with someone before using it at a meeting where the pattern you are focusing on changing is likely to be repeated.

2] 5 minutes – Use your completed script.

3] 15 minutes – Group discussion.

4] Record insight, feedback you received and how you felt. Make note of your ideas about how to use the script in different settings (e.g., performance discussions, coaching and/or mentoring conversations or as a part of a mini skill-building presentation, etc.).

IT HAPPENS EVERYDAY

PATTERN SCRIPT FOR STEP 1 ABOVE

Step P1:
I have noticed several patterns *(no more than 3)* at our meetings. The most recent example happened *(when)*. I didn't say anything at the time but as of today I *(state the action you want to take and/or the feelings you had)*.

Step P2:
I want your support to *(examples: interrupt, stop, point out, acknowledge, etc. Choose one of the examples or insert your own)* this pattern because it *(describe what you perceive as its impact on the quality of the meeting and the work done by meeting participants. You might also include a short list of the longer-term impacts you see)*.

Step P3:
You can help me by *(be concise and specific about 2 or 3 things the meeting attendees can do)*.

Step P4:
I appreciate your listening. Are you willing to help me? *(Wait for their response and clarify your request if necessary.)*

Step P5:
When will you start?

Step P6:
Here's what I am committed to do *(list 2 or 3 things that will support and/or challenge them)*.

Step P7:
Thanks, I'm ready to *(what?)*.

APPENDICES

KEY CONCEPTS

European-American or American White Male Culture
Culture describes shared values and beliefs of a group. U.S. American white male culture is interesting in that it can be seen and described by those who are not members of the culture yet, for many white men the characteristics they share with other white men are most often invisible. This stems in part from the fact that most white men rarely have to step out of their culture, while many white women and people of color learn to be bi-cultural, often moving in and out of white male culture on a daily basis. The paradox is that in order for one to best understand one's culture, one has to leave it.

The shared characteristics of white men in the United States determine, in large part, how things get done and the norms of interaction, both business and personal. Within a culture, individuals will vary in their knowledge, acceptance and support of the culture. Some won't know they are members of a group with a distinct culture. There are six themes of the U.S. white male culture we engage in our work:

- Rugged individualism
- Low tolerance for uncertainty and ambiguity
- Focus on action over reflection (doing over being)
- Rationality over emotion (head over heart)
- Time as linear and future focused
- Status and rank over connection

The cultural literature often refers to the above characteristics as "American Culture" while at the same time identifying African American, Asian American and other ethnic subcultures of the U.S. as something else. The white male facet of what is simply described as American Culture often goes unspoken and remains invisible.

Since most organizations and institutions in the U.S. are based on white male cultural values such as those listed above, all of us — white men, white women, and people of color — have learned to operate in this culture.

A brief note about the words we use. Technically speaking the term European-American refers more to ethnicity and region of origin, while the terms white and male refer more to race and gender, respectively. We have chosen to describe the above culture more often as white male culture in the U.S. in part because we have found many white men tend to more easily identify themselves as white male than European-American. Please use the term you most prefer.

Partnership and Partnership Culture

Partner: A person associated with another or member of a business partnership.

Have you ever felt like a child at work? Have you ever wondered why your manager thought you needed to be protected from what everyone knew was coming (downsizing, a merger, plant closings, a new CEO, etc.)? When you have that feeling or are asking similar questions, you are probably responding to the parental nature of organizations. Most organizations are hierarchical and depend on predictability, and command and control, to meet business goals. Another way to think about the parental nature of organizations is to view them as patriarchal – or "father knows best." Patriarchy is different than building a diversity partnership culture in our organizations. Peter Block dedicates Chapter Two of his 1993 book, *Stewardship*, to partnership as an alternative to patriarchy. We believe that diversity partnerships are on the cutting edge of changing organizations. Block describes partnership as having four requirements that need to be demonstrated for real partnership to develop. His requirements fit the intention of White Men As Full Diversity Partners®' diversity partnership work.

Block's four requirements for real partnership include:
- Exchange of purpose – "Purpose gets defined through dialogue." (Block, 1993 p. 29)
- Right to say no – "If we cannot say no, then saying yes has no meaning." (p. 30)
- Joint accountability – Each person is responsible for outcomes and the current situation. "If people in organizations want the freedom partnership offers, the price of that freedom is to take personal accountability for the success and failure of our unit and our community." (p. 30)
- Absolute honesty – It's essential for partnership. (p. 30)

Crutch-Free Diversity Partnership Framework

- Our respective roles are clear and we understand them rather than assuming what we each mean. I ask before assuming I know.

- We agree on how we will engage conflict.

- We actively apply and live in the key paradoxes. Individually, we take time to find out whether our perspectives match, or not. We look at how each of us uses the paradoxes – how we demonstrate them in our behavior.

- We use frequent direct feedback about what works in the partnership and what doesn't work. We listen to understand. We talk about how the contributions we make to our partnership affect our commitment to our work and each other.

- We acknowledge the steps we've taken to support and challenge each other. We recognize that our diversity partners may have very different views and understandings of the issues we are facing together. We acknowledge that our frames of reference have been affected by differences of gender, race, class, sexual orientation, experience, etc. It's our job to understand each other's world views and their influence on how we work together.

- We show respect for each other in the moment…when it counts. Some of these moments will occur when our partner is not present. These will be opportunities we can use to demonstrate respect for our partner and our partnership.

- We attend to a broken trust between us, rather than assume that our partnership is a lost cause. "Once broken, never regained," is unacceptable as our first response. Tears in the fabric of our partnership are used to test our commitment, demonstrate tenacity and build skill. We refuse to hold on to misunderstandings. We do that by scheduling time to air and resolve misunderstandings.

Paradox

The American Heritage Dictionary of the English Language defines paradox as a seemingly contradictory statement that may nonetheless be true. Another of its definitions suggests that paradox can and does live in an individual, group, situation or action that exhibits inexplicable or contradictory aspects.

Contradictions often contain conflict, particularly when the contradictions co-exist at the same time in the same individual, group and/or situation. Diversity partnership is a hotbed of paradox. We offer four that show up repeatedly in diversity partnership work that require conscious attention and skill building. Diversity partners build skill at living with paradox and conflict. Kenwyn K. Smith and David N. Berg describe paradox in detail in their book, *Paradoxes of Group Life*.

Paradox #1 – Individual/Group:

White men are *both* individuals *and* members of the white male group. When white men acknowledge their membership in the white male group, they do not give up their individuality.

Example:
"Don't lump me in with other white guys. Maybe I'm different."
"I've never thought of myself as being a member of a white male group, and I am."

Paradox #2 – Difference/Sameness

A deeper picture of diversity requires both a focus on difference *and* sameness, diversity *and* commonality. Each can only be defined in terms of the other. For example, being color-conscious *and* color-blind simultaneously.

Example:
"I treat everyone the same. I don't see color."
"I want my coworkers to see my color. It's an important part of me."

Paradox #3 – Support/Challenge

Breakthrough learning is created by diversity partners who support *and* challenge each other. Partners do not choose one or the other side of this or any paradox. Both sides are necessary in effective results-focused diversity partnerships.

Example:
"We need to be patient and understanding here…let people come along at their own pace."
"That behavior is wrong and it must change."

Paradox #4 – No Fault/Responsibility:

It is not my fault *and* I am responsible. Often white men feel they are being asked to carry the personal burden of the historical mistreatment of other groups. It is not our fault and we are vital parts of the dialogue needed to create more equitable systems for everyone, including white men.

Example:
"I didn't create this situation…and I can and will look at my responsibility for keeping it in place."

Difficult Conversations

A difficult conversation is any conversation you find hard to initiate, participate in and complete. Difficult conversations require preparation. The ability to engage in difficult conversations is a key concept of diversity partnership work.*

Difficult conversations have three parts:

1. **Content:** What is it you want to talk about? What are your intentions for discussing it?

2. **Feelings:** What are you feeling as you prepare for the conversation? It does little good to attempt to hide or bury your feelings.

3. **The identity conversation:** How does this situation threaten our sense of who we are?

Preparation:

- Uncover your assumptions and *intentions* before you schedule time for the conversation.

- Don't assume you know your partner's intentions. You don't.

- Difficult conversations require risk-taking; take some.

*This material has been adapted from the book *Difficult Conversations*.

GLOSSARY

Systemic Privilege/Advantage
Systemic privilege is the unspoken and unacknowledged benefits that come to a person through no virtue of their own but are made to look normal and available to any person who wants them. These benefits are often invisible to those who receive them and clearly visible to those who don't.

Classism
Classism is prejudice and/or discrimination, either personal or institutional, against people because of their real or perceived economic status or background. *(http://cluh2.tripod.com/definitions.html#classism)*

Collusion
Collusion is the often unconscious actions that reinforce/support the status quo that benefit some at the expense of others. Collusion can be conscious or unconscious, active or passive.

Heterosexism
Heterosexism is action taken to limit people's rights and privileges or access to them, based on the conscious or unconscious belief or opinion that heterosexuality is the normal and right expression of sexuality and any other expression is abnormal and wrong. The privileges and rights that are denied can be legislative, public and familial.

Fluid Identity
Fluid Identity is the concept that identity is not rigid but can and does change. This idea is often used in terms of gender, sexuality, and race, as well as other factors of identity. This concept is fundamentally contrary to binary systems. A person who feels her/his identity is fluid often believes that rigid categories are oppressive and incapable of accurately describing her/his experience and identities. *(http://cluh2.tripod.com/)*

Homophobia
Homophobia is the fear or hatred of gays, lesbians, or queer-identified people in general. It can be manifested as an intense dislike or rejection of such people, or violent actions against them. *(http://cluh2.tripod.com/definitions.html)*
See the definition of Heterosexism, above.

Sex Reassignment Surgery (SRS)

SRS is the surgical procedure to modify one's primary sexual characteristics (genitalia) from those of one sex to those of the opposite sex. SRS may also include secondary surgery such as breast augmentation or reduction and/or removing the Adam's apple. *(http://www.tg2tg.org/forums/lifestyles)*

SOFFA

A SOFFA is a Significant Other, Friend, Family, or Ally of a transsexual, transgender, inter-sex or other gender-variant person. *(http://www.virtualcity.com/)*

Transgender (TG)

Transgender is a more recently adopted umbrella term that includes all persons who engage in cross-gender activities or lifestyles regardless of motivation or sexual orientation. *(http://www.tg2tg.org/forums/lifestyles)*

Transsexual* (TS)

Transsexual describes an individual whose gender identity is the opposite of his or her physical sex. Typically such individuals desire modification of their physical body (i.e., SRS) to match their gender identity, and derive no "thrill," erotic or otherwise, from merely wearing the clothing associated with the opposite biological gender. *(http://www.tg2tg.org/forums/lifestyles)*

* Transsexual may also be spelled transexual, depending on country of origin. *(http://pages.sbcglobal.net/texasrat/page9.html)*

White Guilt

White guilt is a frequent response of white people to learning about white privilege. White guilt makes white individuals feel shameful about the history of oppression of people of color and the role white persons have played in perpetuating that system, as well as their individual complicity with that system. *(http://cluh2.tripod.com/definitions.html)*

SUGGESTED READING:

Arrien, Angeles. *The Four-Fold Way: Walking the Paths of the Warrior, Teacher, Healer, and Visionary.* HarperSanFrancisco: 1993. ISBN: 0-06-250059-7

Bilodeau, M.S., Lorrainne. *The Anger Workbook.* MIF Books: 1992. ISBN: 1-56731-202-0

Block, Peter. *Stewardship.* Berrett Koehler: 1993. ISBN: 1-881052-28-1

Bridges, William. *Managing Transitions, Making The Most of Change.* Addison Wesley: 1991. ISBN: 0-201-55073-3

Cashman, Kevin. *Leadership from the Inside Out.* Executive Excellence Publishing: 1998. ISBN: 1-890009-29-6

Dana, Daniel, Ph.D, *Managing Differences: How to Build Better Relationships at Work and Home.* MTI Publications: 1997. ISBN: 0-9621534-3-5

Goleman, Daniel, Richard Boyatzis, and Annie McKee. *Primal Leadership: Realizing The Power Of Emotional Intelligence.* Harvard Business School Press: 2002. ISBN:1-57851-486-X

Johnson, Barry. *Polarity Management: Identifying and Managing Unsolvable Problems.* Human Resource Development Press: 1992. ISBN: 0-87425-176-1

Lukeman, Alex and Gayle. *Beyond Blame: Reclaiming The Power You Give To Others.* North Star Publications: 1997. ISBN: 1-880823-14-4

Maurer, Rick. *Feedback Toolkit: 16 Tools for Better Communication in the Workplace.* Productivity Press: 1994. ISBN:1-56327-056-0

McGraw, Phillip C., Ph.D. *Life Strategies: Doing What Works, Doing What Matters.* Hyperion: 1999. ISBN: 0-7868-8459-2

Pfeffer, Jeffrey. *Managing with Power: Politics and Influence in Organizations.* Harvard Business School Press: 1992. ISBN: 0-87584-314-X

Scott, Susan. *Fierce Conversations: Achieving Success at Work & in Life, One Conversation at a Time.* Berkley Books: 2002. ISBN: 0-425-19337-3

Stone, Douglas, Bruce Patton and Sheila Heen. *Difficult Conversations: How to Discuss What Matters Most.* Penguin Books: 2000. ISBN: 0-14-028852 X

Takaki, Ronald. *From Different Shores: Perspectives on Race and Ethnicity in America.* Second Edition. Oxford University Press: 1994. ISBN: 0-19-508368-7

Takaki, Ronald. *A Different Mirror: A History of Multicultural America,* 1993. ISBN: 0-316-83111-5

Wheatley, Margaret, J. *Leadership and the New Science: Discovering Order in a Chaotic World.* Berrett-Koehler Publishers: 1999. ISBN: 1-57675-055-8

Whyte, David. *The Heart Aroused: Poetry and the Preservation of the Soul in Corporate America.* Revised Edition. Doubleday: 2002. ISBN 0-385-48418-6

Wylie, Pete, Dr., and Dr. Mardy Grothe. *Can This Partnership Be Saved? Improving (or Salvaging) Your Key Business Relationships.* Upstart Publishing Company, Inc.: 1993. ISBN: 0-936894-42-3

www.wmfdp.com
See the Online Resources page.

Diversity Partnership Tips for White Men: A Skills Building Field Guide

By Bill Proudman, Michael Welp, Jo Ann Morris

At last, a book that puts the invisible partners of diversity – white men – in the spotlight. This paradigm-busting field guide invites white men to step out of the shadows and fully join their organizations' diversity efforts. Because, contrary to popular belief, their engagement is critical to the success of any serious diversity initiative. Only when white men form vital partnerships with other white men, white women and people of color can organizations move from mere pro forma head count increases to a genuinely new, inclusive culture. Part of the challenge is understanding where white men are coming from. You'll learn what white male culture is, and how it affects the white man's business success. And you may be surprised to find out that despite their dominant position, white men are often overtly excluded from mainstream diversity efforts. That's not a good thing, because there are powerful reasons why white men should care about – and invest in – diversity initiatives (hint: the stakes are much higher than most white men realize). Choosing to get involved in diversity actually helps white men build leadership skills; we'll show you how. Plus, we outline new ways to smash old barriers so white men can partner more effectively with others.

$15.95 ISBN 0-9754192-1-8

order books at www.wmfdp.com

Eight Critical Leadership Skills Created Through Effective Diversity Partnerships: A Skills Building Field Guide

By Michael Welp, Jo Ann Morris, Bill Proudman

The secret is out: While there's no shortage of business leadership programs to sign up for, they may not be the best places to build the complex skills you need to effectively lead in today's complex workplaces. This landmark field guide brings the most sought-after talents right to your doorstep. You'll learn how real leadership is best cultivated: by working with the diverse people around you. As you read and reflect on the thought-provoking questions and do the activities described, you'll boost your ability to lead – and improve your organization's business results.

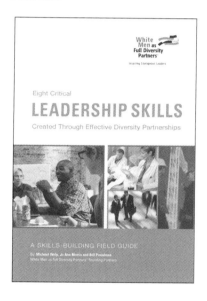

We consider such defining questions as: What is courage? Where does it come from? And why do you need it at work? You'll find out how to escape the all-too-common trap of simplistic either/or thinking and embrace the normal paradoxes of every workplace – so you can work with reality instead of against it. Using our roadmap for difficult conversations, you'll learn about the detours, dangers and delays you're likely to encounter so you can anticipate and overcome them. In the same vein, we show you how to stay on your intended path through periods of change by allowing for the inevitable turbulence, uncertainty and resistance. And, not least, we explore how you can develop a fuller and deeper kind of leadership by connecting your head and your heart.

$15.95 ISBN 0-9754192-0-X

order books at www.wmfdp.com

AUTHOR BIOGRAPHIES

JO ANN MORRIS is a founding partner of White Men as Full Diversity Partners®. She is an executive coach and organization change consultant. Her practice is noted for its Integral Coaching methods for executives and Diversity In-depth Coaching.

Jo Ann was an Information Technology and Programming Manager for 15 years prior to WMFDP. Jo Ann's most challenging technology position was with Fidelity Mutual funds. She was their software programming manager.

She has been a guest lecturer at the Lyndon Baines Johnson Public Executive Institute at the University of Texas at Austin and at the Brandeis University Women in Management Program. She has designed and facilitated diversity initiatives with clients ranging from The Greater Greensboro North Carolina Chamber of Commerce, Exxon Chemicals and Lucent Technologies to the General Services Administration and American Express. *She lives in Connecticut and can be reached at 202.352.4776 or morris@wmfdp.com.*

BILL PROUDMAN is a founding partner of White Men as Full Diversity Partners®, a consulting firm that develops courageous leaders who build effective partnerships between white men, white women, and men and women of color in organizations. He pioneered white-male-only learning labs in the mid-90s after noticing that white male leaders repeatedly disengaged from diversity efforts, almost always looking to white women, and men and women of color, to lead and educate. This provocative work became the seed for his involvement in the creation of WMFDP.

Bill remains an avid diversity learner and an impassioned believer that everyone has a role to play to create just and equitable communities and organizations. He has 25 years experience as a process facilitator and consultant working on the human side of organizational change and transformation. Bill has been an ongoing consultant to the American Leadership Forum having designed and conducted numerous residential leadership development programs since the early 90s. *Bill splits time between homes in Portland, Oregon and the southern Cascades of Washington State. He can be reached at 503-281-5585 or proudman@wmfdp.com.*

MICHAEL WELP, PH.D. is a founding partner of White Men as Full Diversity Partners®. Known for his authentic, trust-building style, Michael works to develop leadership in everyone. Michael has facilitated interracial teambuilding for South African corporations, and has authored a dissertation and book chapter about white men and diversity. An adjunct faculty at the Capella University, he is the recipient of the Minnesota Organization Development Practitioner of the Year Award and is a professional member of NTL Institute for Applied Behavioral Science. Michael also founded EqualVoice, an organization development consulting firm known for building collaborative work cultures and for its transformative approaches to conflict. *He lives in Sandpoint, Idaho and can be reached at 208.263.6775 or welp@wmfdp.com.*

ABOUT WMFDP

White Men as Full Diversity Partners® is a culture-change consulting firm. We offer coaching, curriculum design, learning lab intensives and system-wide change opportunities to inspire organizational leadership to make commitments, and to operate with courage when addressing issues related to inclusion and diversity. The leading edge of diversity work involves white men, white women and people of color, partnering with each other to move white men from the sidelines of diversity efforts – to being fully in the midst of these efforts at all levels of the organization. In the end we do three things: build skills, transform mindsets, and create powerful partnerships within the organizations we serve. Visit our website for more about WMFDP.

www.wmfdp.com